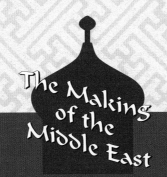

The Making of the Middle East

The Middle East
in the
Age of Uncertainty
1991-Present

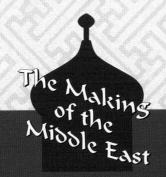

The Middle East
in the
Age of Uncertainty
1991-Present

Barry Rubin

Mason Crest Publishers
Philadelphia

Frontispiece: A U.S. Air Force loadmaster drops critical supplies to replenish U.S. ground forces in Afghanistan.

Produced by OTTN Publishing, Stockton, N.J.

Mason Crest Publishers
370 Reed Road
Broomall, PA 19008
www.masoncrest.com

First printing

1 3 5 7 9 8 6 4 2

Library of Congress Cataloging-in-Publication Data

Rubin, Barry M.
  The Middle East in the age of uncertainty, 1991–present / Barry Rubin.
      p. cm. — (The making of the Middle East)
  Includes bibliographical references and index.
  ISBN-13: 978-1-4222-0176-3
  ISBN-10: 1-4222-0176-7
  1. Middle East—History—1979—Juvenile literature. I. Title.
  DS44R83 2007
  956.05'3—dc22
                                    2007024532

Arab-Israeli Relations, 1950–1979

The Arabian Peninsula in the Age of Oil

The Cold War in the Middle East, 1950–1991

The Iranian Revolution and the Resurgence of Islam

The Middle East in the Age of Uncertainty, 1991–Present

The Ottoman and Qajar Empires in the Age of Reform

The Palestine Mandate and the Creation of Israel, 1920–1949

The Rise of Nationalism: The Arab World, Turkey, and Iran

Tensions in the Gulf, 1978–1991

Table of Contents

Introduction:
The Importance of the Middle East

The region known as the Middle East has a significant impact on world affairs. The countries of the greater Middle East—the Arab states of the Arabian Peninsula, Eastern Mediterranean, and North Africa, along with Israel, Turkey, Iran, and Afghanistan—possess a large portion of the world's oil, a valuable commodity that is the key to modern economies. The region also gave birth to three of the world's major faiths: Judaism, Christianity, and Islam.

In recent years it has become obvious that events in the Middle East affect the security and prosperity of the rest of the world. But although such issues as the wars in Iraq and Afghanistan, the floundering Israeli-Palestinian peace process, and the struggles within countries like Lebanon and Sudan are often in the news, few Americans understand the turbulent history of this region.

Human civilization in the Middle East dates back more than 8,000 years, but in many cases the modern conflicts and issues in the region can be attributed to events and decisions made during the past 150 years. In particular, after World War I ended in 1918, the victorious Allies—especially France and Great Britain—redrew the map of the Middle East, creating a number of new countries, such as Iraq, Jordan, and Syria. Other states, such as Egypt and Iran, were dominated by foreign powers until after the Second World War. Many of the Middle Eastern countries did not become independent until the 1960s or 1970s. Political and economic developments in the Middle Eastern states over the past four decades have shaped the region's direction and led to today's headlines.

The purpose of the MAKING OF THE MIDDLE EAST series is to nurture a better understanding of this critical region, by providing the basic history along

with explanation and analysis of trends, decisions, and events. Books will examine important movements in the Middle East, such as the development of nationalism in the 1880s and the rise of Islamism from the 1970s to the present day.

The 10 volumes in the MAKING OF THE MIDDLE EAST series are written in clear, accessible prose and are illustrated with numerous historical photos and maps. The series should spark students' interest, providing future decision-makers with a solid foundation for understanding an area of critical importance to the United States and the world.

Two scenes from the Gulf War of 1991. (Opposite) A destroyed Iraqi tank burns in the desert. (Right) Coalition soldiers and Kuwaiti civilians celebrate the end of the Iraqi occupation, Kuwait City.

1 Overview

*E*vents in 1991 seemed to augur a new era in the troubled history of the modern Middle East. The key development was the expulsion of one Arab state's army from the land of an Arab neighbor it had invaded—an expulsion effected by a U.S.-led military coalition that included armed forces from still other Arab states.

On August 2, 1990, the armed forces of Iraq had invaded and quickly overrun the small but oil-rich emirate of Kuwait. Four days later, the United Nations Security Council, meeting in an emergency session, demanded the "immediate and unconditional" withdrawal of all Iraqi forces from Kuwait and imposed a trade embargo on Iraq. Iraqi dictator

9

Saddam Hussein was not moved: on August 8, Iraq announced that it had annexed Kuwait.

Operation Desert Shield

Around the same time, the United States initiated Operation Desert Shield. U.S. troops began deploying to northern Saudi Arabia at the request of that country's rulers, who were concerned that Saddam Hussein might have further territorial ambitions.

Over the following weeks and months, the international community mobilized to reverse Iraq's aggression. By the end of August, the U.N. Security Council had authorized the use of force to compel Iraqi compliance with its resolutions, and in late November the Security Council voted to impose a deadline of January 15, 1991, for Iraq's withdrawal from Kuwait. Meanwhile, the United States had assembled a large international coalition to oppose Iraq. It included military contingents from such influential Arab states as Egypt and Syria.

Efforts to resolve the crisis through diplomacy—including initiatives by the Soviet Union's leader, Mikhail Gorbachev—proved futile. The Security Council's January 15 deadline came and went.

The Gulf War and its Aftermath

Operation Desert Storm, the coalition's code name for the military effort to expel Iraq from Kuwait, began on January 17 with predawn air strikes. For the next five weeks, coalition bombers and cruise missiles pounded targets inside Iraq and Iraqi troop concentrations in Kuwait.

In the aftermath of the Gulf War, Saddam Hussein brutally repressed uprisings by Shia in the south and Kurds in the north. Here, displaced Kurds seek refuge near the border with Turkey.

Then, on February 24, coalition armored units—the majority of them American—streamed across the Saudi border into Kuwait and western Iraq. Coalition forces quickly overwhelmed the Iraqis. In just 100 hours of fighting, more than 70,000 Iraqi soldiers surrendered, and at least 25,000 were killed. Coalition battle deaths in the Gulf War, meanwhile, totaled 240.

Iraqi forces had been chased from Kuwait, and that country's government had returned from exile. Although Saddam Hussein remained in power in Iraq, U.S. leaders decided against marching all the way to Baghdad to overthrow his regime. Regime change in Iraq had not been a stated objective of the war, and American officials feared that the Arab members of the coalition would not support this action. On February 28 a cease-fire announced by U.S. president George H. W. Bush went into effect.

During the first week of March, as coalition and Iraqi commanders met to discuss the terms for a permanent cease-fire, Kurds in northern Iraq and Shia Muslims in the southern part of the country were rising up against Saddam's regime. The Iraqi dictator's days appeared numbered.

The Gulf War, which appeared to be an unqualified success, was a high-water mark for cooperation between the nations of the West and the Middle East, and for U.S. influence in the region. American policymakers, along with many analysts, saw hope for a new era in the Middle East. Arab regimes seemed ready to abandon policies that had contributed to decades of strife, suffering, and defeat and to chart a course of moderation, pragmatism, modernization, and reform. The collapse of the Soviet Union, which would be complete by the end of 1991, not only removed the remnants of U.S.-Soviet competition in the Middle East but also seemed to confirm the advantages of an open society, a free-enterprise economy, and a democratic political system. The time seemed right for compromise—even with Israel—to resolve the region's outstanding problems.

Ultimately, this optimistic vision did not come to pass, as diplomatic, social, and economic progress in the Middle East proved elusive. Autocratic Arab governments held on to power, and often used radical Arab nationalism and other extremist ideologies to conceal their failures.

Indeed, in the aftermath of the Gulf War, the problems of the Middle East arguably deepened. Saddam Hussein ruthlessly suppressed the Shia and Kurdish uprisings, and his regime continued to bedevil the international community and worry his neighbors in the region. Militant Islam in Iran was also a threat. The Arab-Israeli conflict remained unresolved.

Hopes that the Israeli-Palestinian conflict would be resolved after the Gulf War ultimately did not pan out. In this February 2007 photo, Palestinian youths throw rocks at Israeli soldiers patrolling the West Bank town of Ramallah.

Despite the high hopes and expectations of 1991, the Middle East more than 15 years later continues to be deadlocked in a stagnant system. The paradox is that social and economic progress, democracy, peace, and an end to violent turmoil are all linked together in requiring a fundamental change in the region's political structure. Yet this is no easy task. The existing system is deeply entrenched, enjoying not only power but also a large degree of mass support. To intensify the problem, the main alternative being offered to the existing situation is radical Islamism, which creates only more disorder and whose triumph might worsen the region's difficulties. There are no easy ways out of this trap.

(Opposite) Palestinians protest U.S. policy in Iraq, 2004. (Right) Iraqi dictator Saddam Hussein was a source of instability in the Persian Gulf.

2 The Challenge of the Modern Era

he central problem of Arab and Muslim societies during the past century has been the gap between expectations and reality. In contrast to the bright future promised by Arab nationalists, the modern history of the Middle East has been largely a story of Arab defeat and failure. The attempt to change that basic paradigm in the 1990s would be thwarted by the same issues and ideas that had so long troubled the Arab world.

The Limits of Pan-Arab Nationalism

The internal failures of the Arab world can be attributed to both the misrule of individual regimes and the counterproductive efforts to bring about pan-Arab unity. For a very long time, Arab nationalism had been the Arab world's leading ideology. Yet this very structure of Arab politics inspired constant battles between states as they sought to dominate or escape domination by other countries.

Shaped by the belief that one state, leader, and idea could dominate the region, the Arab world plunged itself into repeated crises that produced misery, defeat, and stunted development. Gamal Abdel Nasser, Egypt's president, tried and failed to unite the Arab world through subversive persuasion in the 1950s and 1960s. Beginning in the 1980s, the Iraqi dictator Saddam Hussein sought to claim the mantle of Arab leadership, provoking a brutal eight-year-long war with Iran. Yet in all the years up to the 1990s, proper ideology—not material success—was seen as the measure of both doctrines and leaders. For example, though Nasser's ambitions and errors cost his country huge casualties and financial losses, he remained a hero to many throughout the Arab world.

Arab candidates for regional power (or subregional domination) and their smaller neighbors waged a costly, sometimes catastrophic, struggle in which tens of thousands of people died, massive resources were wasted, economic development was slowed, and living standards were held back. Contrary to Arab nationalism's demands and promises, the West was not expelled, and Israel was not destroyed. Progress toward democracy stagnated, and Arab intellectual life was crippled by these obsessions. The Palestinian cause—supposedly the focus and beneficiary of Arab cooperation—became an arena for this competition, which inevitably delayed a solution to the conflict.

But while Arab nationalism failed, it was not displaced as the organizing principle of the Arab world. Instead, the drive to impose Arab brotherhood and homogeneity brought constant quarrels and splits, intensifying interstate conflict. For the idea that there should be one leader of the Arabs or of the region as a whole inevitably ignited rivalries, including those between Iraq and Iran, Syria and Iraq, Egypt and Saudi Arabia, and Syria and Jordan. Arab states took different sides—or at least espoused conflicting strategies—on every issue. Even when they reached joint decisions, they were notoriously unable to implement them. During the Cold War, they called in competing patrons, the United States and the Soviet Union, to fight their local battles.

What pan-Arab nationalism really did was to furnish a popular ideological cover for nation-state imperialism, resulting in a failure to create the kind of stable states and regional system necessary for successful development. Arab regimes interfered in each other's internal affairs, sponsoring political factions and terrorist groups. There were civil wars in Yemen, Sudan, Algeria, Lebanon, and Iraq. Syria and Libya supported non-Arab Iran in its war against Iraq. Even the Iraqi and Syrian branches of the Baath Party bickered over which was the proper leader. Libya's dictator Muammar Qadhafi, whose claim to leadership sometimes qualified as comic relief, stirred up deadly mischief everywhere.

Bad Governance

The governments of every Arab state failed domestically to produce good administration, democratic government, or rapid economic development (except in those cases of relatively unpopulated states with vast oil resources). At the same time, the regimes were brilliant at continuing to hold on to power despite their failures. Whether their orientation was more radical nationalist (Egypt, Syria, Iraq, Libya) or traditionalist (Morocco, Jordan, Saudi Arabia), the governments were repressive and riddled with corruption, inefficiency, and incompetence. They generally proved unable to reform or improve themselves.

If anything, the "progressive" dictatorships often proved worse than the "reactionary" monarchies. Where coups did take place—as in Egypt, Syria, Libya, and Iraq—the resulting regimes were also far from satisfactory and certainly failed to keep their promises of rapid development, inter-Arab cooperation, or military triumphs. They were considerably more repressive than the kingdoms they replaced and did not necessarily do a better job of governing. On the positive side, they did carry out land reform programs and empowered some additional social groups. But they also came to embody the problems of incompetence and corruption they were supposed to solve. A highly symbolic last straw was when Syria's president Hafez al-Assad died and, in monarchical style, was succeeded by his son.

Conflict with Israel

Since Israel's founding in 1948, the Arab states and the Palestinian movement proved unable to defeat—much less destroy—the Jewish state.

Instead, Israel became stronger while Arab armies suffered a string of military defeats, in 1956 (the Suez Crisis), 1967 (the Six-Day War), and 1973 (the October, or Yom Kippur, War). Violence and threats did not even dislodge

Supporters of Algeria's Islamic Salvation Front (FIS) at a May 1991 rally in Algiers. Later in the year, the FIS triumphed in parliamentary elections, but the Algerian military nullified the results, triggering a long and bloody civil war.

Israel from the territories it captured from Arab neighbors during the Six-Day War, including the Gaza Strip, captured from Egypt; the Golan Heights, captured from Syria; and the West Bank, captured from Jordan. The costs of continuing the conflict with Israel damaged Arab interests and weakened Arab states. Moreover, the conflict divided Arab states even further as each regime and movement manipulated the issue to promote its interests, mobilize domestic support, and gain an edge over rivals.

Other related problems included Jordan's brief civil war (1970) and Lebanon's long civil war (1975–1990); the Arab boycott of Egypt after the Camp David peace agreement of 1978; Arab states' rivalry in trying to control the Palestine Liberation Organization (PLO); and the assassinations of Jordan's King Abdullah I (1951) and Egyptian president Anwar el-Sadat (1981).

The conflict with Israel and the question of a homeland for Palestinians became a handy tool by which every ruler could justify virtually any policy. Democracy, economic reform, and other long-needed changes could be declared impossible to consider under the endless conditions of war. The Israel issue was the opiate of the Arab world, an addiction that provided false satisfaction and distraction to the masses while intoxicating the rulers and elites to the point that they could not perform well. The conflict drew Arab countries into losing wars, provided a rationale for dictatorship, justified counterproductive economic and social policies, and inhibited necessary cooperation with the United States. It fostered revolutionary Islamic movements, expensive arms races, and catastrophic civil wars.

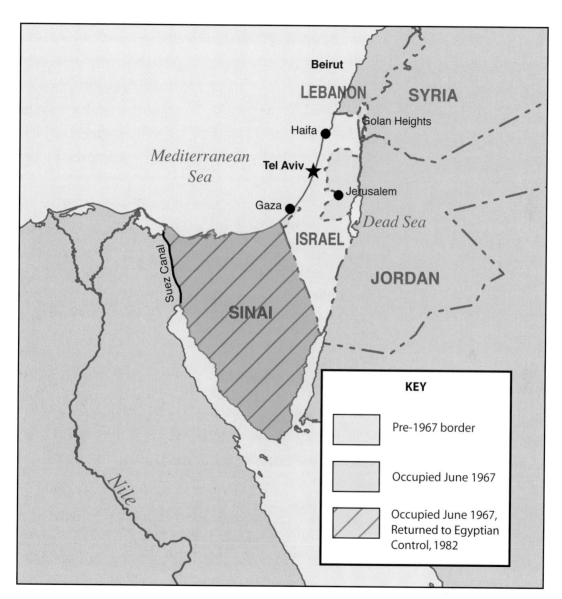

Israeli territorial gains as a result of the Six-Day War.

The Persistent Influence of the West

Efforts to eliminate Western influence—a long-standing dream of many Arabs—did not succeed. Indeed, given globalization, the Western cultural presence actually increased in the Arab world. Even Islamist Iran could not keep out American entertainment and fashions. On the political level, too, Arab states brought in Western forces to help them. From the 1950s to the 1980s, the radical states sought Soviet help to increase their regional leverage, fight Israel, and combat the moderate states. The moderates turned to the United States to arm and save them. The monarchies of the Persian Gulf asked the United States to convoy their oil tankers, sell them arms, and protect them from Iran during the 1980s. During the following decade, the Arab world turned to the United States to save Kuwait and then to act as broker in an Arab-Israeli peace process.

Insecurity in the Persian Gulf

The Arab states failed to maintain peace or security in the Persian Gulf. As a result, two bloody wars—the Iran-Iraq War of 1980–1988 and the Gulf War of 1991—caused immense losses to life and property, wasted tens of billions of dollars that could have been used to raise living standards, and endangered the very survival of countries in the region. Middle Eastern arms races also cost tens of billions of additional dollars that could have been better used. This problem was rooted in Iraqi aggression, fueled and legitimized by pan-Arab ideology; Iranian ambitions, stimulated and magnified by Islamist doctrine; and the readiness of the Arab monarchies of the Persian Gulf to appease Iraq, combined with their reluctance to seek Western help sufficient to deter would-be attackers.

Islamism: No Panacea

Islamist ideologies failed as badly as their Arab nationalist predecessors. There were no successful Islamist revolts in Arab states, and even the one existing Islamist regime, in Iran, lost the support of the masses there. Radical Islamism certainly did pose a threat to the existing order. Iran sponsored subversive and terrorist groups in the Persian Gulf, Lebanon, and among the Palestinians. In every country, too, Islamist groups arose and became the principal opposition movements, staging full-scale revolts in Egypt and Algeria. Often—though by no means always—they contributed new dimensions of violence and instability to the already existing heap of problems confronting the region. Islamists became strong voices opposing democracy and needed social reforms. In short, Islamist groups generally made things worse rather than better.

Sailors at the bow of the USS *Kidd*, a guided-missile destroyer, watch reflagged Kuwaiti oil tankers sailing through the Persian Gulf during the Iran-Iraq War.

Stunted Development

For decades, the Arab world has been plagued by a slow, even stagnant, pace of economic development. If not for the existence of oil and natural gas—

obviously a very considerable advantage but one that nonetheless has limits—virtually every Arab country would be an economic basket case. In many countries, radical rule wasted huge resources through warfare and through adherence to rigid but failing domestic policies. Dictatorship has remained the principal type of government in the Arab world at a time when other developing regions are overwhelmingly turning toward more democracy, civil liberties, and human rights—all of which can help attract investment and accelerate economic performance.

Over the past decades, several trends have contributed to the Middle East's dismal economic outlook. According to the World Bank, sub-Saharan Africa is the only region in the world that has seen lower growth in gross domestic product (GDP) and GDP per capita, key indicators of economic performance. Between 1980 and 1990, for example, the Middle East had an average overall GDP growth rate of only 2 percent, compared with 8 percent for East Asia and 5.6 percent for South Asia, two other regions emerging from poverty. In real terms (adjusting for inflation) Arab countries such as Algeria, Jordan, Saudi Arabia, the United Arab Emirates, Iran, Kuwait, Libya, and Iraq experienced no economic growth whatsoever.

Standards of living in much of the Middle East lagged behind other regions of the world in part because of rapid population growth. Where there are more people, economies must produce more jobs, more goods and services, more housing—in short, more wealth—to maintain decent living standards for everyone. Total population in the Middle East and North Africa increased from about 120 million in 1970 to more than 290 million by the end of the century, when approximately 40 percent of the population was 14 years of age or younger. This rapid population growth—in combination with inflation—meant that not even rising prices for crude oil during the period 1970–2000 translated into appreciable gains in per capita income.

Growing urbanization is another trend with significant political implications. People in cities in the Arab world are more exposed to modern thinking, Islamist movements, and cultural contradictions. They seek and receive more education; they require higher levels of jobs and housing. Consequently, they are more likely to have grievances—and to express them. In 1960 only about one in four residents of the Middle East lived in cities; in 2000 the rate approached 6 in 10. With slow growth, low investment, inadequate development of technology, and antiquated government and economic practices, how could there possibly be sufficient jobs, housing, and infrastructure for all these people?

Keeping Power

Despite all the problems in the Arab world, however, existing regimes proved quite adept at staying in power. From the early 1970s to the Gulf War in 1991, no major Arab state witnessed a coup or successful revolution. (Governments were overthrown in Sudan and Yemen, but neither qualifies as a major state.) There is a big difference between the existence of internal conflict or violent opposition and such movements' ability to seize power.

In general, Arab rulers know their own societies well, can assess the relative threats, and are determined to stay in power by whatever means necessary. By 1991 it seemed that, to remain in power, Arab regimes would have to undertake major reforms. Such, however, was not the case.

(Opposite) Under the approving gaze of U.S. president Bill Clinton, Israeli prime minister Yitzhak Rabin and PLO chairman Yasir Arafat shake hands after the signing of the so-called Oslo accord, September 13, 1993. (Right) Muammar Qadhafi, president of Libya. During the 1990s the influence of radical Arab states seemed to be on the wane.

3 1991: The Turning Point That Wasn't

In the aftermath of the Gulf War of 1991, the high cost of pan-Arab nationalism, radical ideology, and militant slogans seemed apparent. Among Arab intellectuals and ordinary citizens alike, there was a growing sense of the futility and wastefulness of the old political ways. A writer in the newspaper *al-Sharq al-Awsat* called the Arab and Islamic world's situation "either a race to suicide or a deliberate plan to exhaust and disarm our nation."

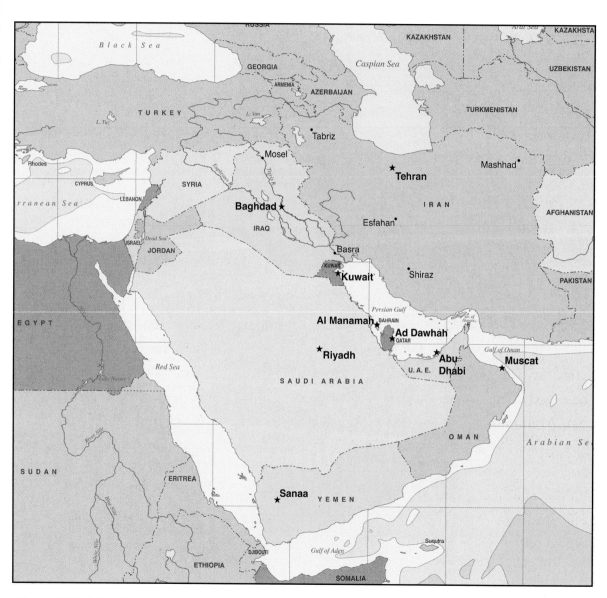

Map of Middle East states, 1991.

In the West, it was widely believed that a major change in the Middle East was inevitable. And it was assumed that pragmatism and material progress would win out over ideology. In the most significant U.S. policy statement explaining this optimism, Tony Lake, President Bill Clinton's national security adviser, said he thought there would be a new era, one in which moderate Middle East states blocked the influence of radical countries and groups. "The extremists will be denied the claim that they are the wave of the future. They will have to confront the reality of their failure [while moderate] governments find the strength to counter extremism at home as well as abroad."

The Coming of "Mideasternism"?

In contrast to Western confidence, Arab weakness and disunity was visible everywhere. With Iraq's defeat, another idol had been toppled—and with remarkable speed and ease. Riyad Najib al-Rayyes wrote in *al-Nahar* that after "two destructive wars . . . a strong united Iraq became a humiliated, besieged and divided Iraq." Egypt's leading newspaper, *al-Ahram*, called pan-Arab nationalists an "extinct Arab tribe." Declarations of dedication to Pan-Arabism, the Palestinian cause, and fighting Israel or America seemed out of fashion. There was talk of such exotic new concepts as "Mideasternism," the idea that all regional peoples—Arabs, Israelis, Turks, and Iranians—should cooperate across national lines, as other areas of the world had done successfully.

Assessing how the Middle East looked in 1991, it is possible to provide a long list of factors that showed the need for massive change and might actually produce such an outcome:

- Long-term, cumulative failures showed Arab leaders and intellectuals that their ideas and politics were not working. This reality seemed to require changes if they were to survive, much less prosper.

- Radical regimes were weaker and more divided than at any time in decades, forcing them to be cautious in bullying neighbors or attacking Western interests. The collapse of the Soviet Union denied them both diplomatic support and low-cost, high-quality weapons. Iran, Iraq, Libya, and Syria were divided by their own diverse ideologies, ambitions, and interests. Iraq had shown itself to be a dangerous bully, threatening Arab interests, while Syria's support for Iran during the Iran-Iraq War undermined its Arab nationalist credentials.

- Moderate states, less intimidated by the weaker radicals, put less emphasis on echoing their ideology and following their leadership. Moderate leaders also saw that they could not buy security by appeasing the radicals. Gulf Arab states were ready to work closely with Washington in order to survive Iraqi, Iranian, and domestic revolutionary threats. Peace, stability, and economic development seemed more desirable ends than an endless struggle risking their prosperity, interests, or even survival.

- Practical self-interest rather than ideology seemed to guide the actions of various Arab governments, which formed alliances with the United States, moved (however haltingly) toward peace with Israel, and eschewed involvement in foreign subversion. While Iraq had claimed its takeover of Kuwait as a victory for Pan-Arabism, most Arab regimes thought its motives were greed and imperialism. Kuwaitis discovered that all their devotion and donations to Arab causes did not shield them from Iraq's invasion, while all their help to the Palestinians did not stop PLO chairman Yasir Arafat from siding with Saddam. In opposing Iraq's aggression, the Arab League—an organization of 22 Arab states—decided to act in the future on the basis of consensus rather than unanimity. Equally, when Egypt, Morocco, Jordan, some Gulf states, or the PLO decided to negotiate with Israel, they were undeterred by criticism that this betrayed Arab nationalist or Islamist principles.

- The United States was now the world's sole superpower. Moderate Arab states had little choice but to maintain good relations with the United States and to use it as a protector, no matter how their public posture differed from that image. Since the United States supported Israel, Arab states saw attacking the latter as too dangerous. Even Syria tried to give the impression in the 1990s that it was cooperating with U.S. efforts to further the Arab-Israeli peace process.

- Given the weakness of the Palestinians' position in the early 1990s (which was partly the result of the shunning of Yasir Arafat by Arab regimes angered at his support for Saddam), it was thought that the PLO would finally adopt a pragmatic policy and make a compromise peace. Israel also seemed ready to make concessions to achieve this goal. For the first time, Arab states and the PLO negotiated seriously with Israel at talks in Madrid, Spain; Washington, D.C.; and Oslo, Norway. The culmination of this process was the Oslo agreement of 1993, which seemed to open the door to peace.

September 9, 1993

Mr. Prime Minister,

The signing of the Declaration of Principles marks a new era in the history of the Middle East. In firm conviction thereof I would like to confirm the following PLO commitments:

The PLO recognizes the right of the State of Israel to exist in peace and security.

The PLO accepts United Nations Security Council Resolutions 242 and 338.

The PLO commits itself to the Middle East peace process, and to a peaceful resolution of the conflict between the two sides and declares that all outstanding issues relating to permanent status will be resolved through negotiations.

The PLO considers that the signing of the Declaration of Principles constitutes a historic event, inaugurating a new epoch of peaceful coexistence, free from violence and all other acts which endanger peace and stability. Accordingly, the PLO renounces the use of terrorism and other acts of violence and will assume responsibility over all PLO elements and personnel in order to assure their compliance, prevent violations and discipline violators.

In view of the promise of a new era and the signing of the Declaration of Principles and based on Palestinian acceptance of Security Council Resolutions 242 and 338, the PLO affirms that those articles of the Palestinian Covenant which deny Israel's right to exist, and the provisions of the Covenant which are inconsistent with the commitments of this letter are now inoperative and no longer valid. Consequently, the PLO undertakes to submit to the Palestinian National Council for formal approval the necessary changes in regard to the Palestinian Covenant.

Sincerely,

Yasser Arafat
Chairman
The Palestine Liberation Organization

9 9 93

Yitzhak Rabin
Prime Minister of Israel

Under the Oslo accords, the PLO recognized—for the first time—Israel's right to exist. PLO chairman Yasir Arafat acknowledged that point in this September 9, 1993, letter to Yitzhak Rabin, Israel's prime minister.

- Arab leaders, along with many ordinary citizens, felt menaced by radical Islamist movements. Most Muslims saw these revolutionary groups as offering strange, even heretical, interpretations of Islam. During the 1990s, Islamists did not take over any Arab governments, and their insurgencies were defeated or contained in Lebanon, Algeria, and Egypt.

- There were hopes that Syria, after participating in the anti-Iraqi coalition in 1991 and negotiating with Israel thereafter, would join the moderate camp.

- There were expectations that Saddam Hussein's regime would remain weak—and perhaps even fall from power—given Iraq's isolation in the Arab world and the international sanctions imposed against the country after the Gulf War, to compel Iraq to disarm.

- The reform movement in Iran, supported by an overwhelming majority of the people, was winning elections. It seemed possible that reformers might take over the government and abandon the Islamist regime's militant policies.

- Calls for reform, democracy, civil society, and other changes toward a more moderate, pragmatic system were starting to be heard in many Arab countries. Lower oil prices in the 1990s made petroleum-producing states nervous about their ability to continue providing domestic privileges to ensure stability. To develop further, the wealthy states needed good relations with the West. Poorer states could not depend on their rich "brothers"—who showed little interest in investing in the Arab world or helping them—and thus hoped to obtain Western aid.

Israel and Jordan concluded a treaty of peace in 1994. Seen here during a signing ceremony at the White House are (seated, from left) King Hussein of Jordan, U.S. president Bill Clinton, and Prime Minister Yitzhak Rabin of Israel.

Promises Unfulfilled

Despite all these factors, the 1990s did not usher in an era of peace, progress, and moderation in the Middle East. The incumbent Arab regimes tended to hedge their bets, viewing fundamental domestic reforms and a resolution of the conflict with Israel as too risky. Leaders saw militancy—at least in verbal form—as insurance against the complaints of their own people or their neighbors. Anti-Americanism was systematically developed, and the PLO and Syria rejected peace with Israel. As for the Islamists, they developed new ideologies and strategies while directing terrorism against the West.

By the early 21st century, virtually none of the problems of the Arab world or Iran had been solved, and remarkably little had changed. The hopes of the 1990s were drowned in developments such as the terrorist attacks on the United States of September 11, 2001; intensified anti-Israel terrorism; the rise of radical jihadism; and waves of anti-American propaganda.

Ultimately, radical Islamists seek to overthrow the regimes of Arab states, which they consider corrupt and un-Islamic. But they have adopted a strategy of waging jihad against foreign enemies. (Opposite) The twin towers of New York City's World Trade Center burn during the al-Qaeda-sponsored attacks of September 11, 2001. (Right) A demonstration in support of Hezbollah, which has fought Israel.

4 *Progress Stifled*

If the events of 1991 began a period of high hopes for change in the Middle East, the most important question is, what went wrong? The answer: just about everything. Briefly, regimes in the region were able to rationalize their failures by blaming Israel, the United States, and the West in general. The regimes in Iran and every Arab state—at the cost of negligible concessions—retained control. They continued to pose as defenders of Islam or of the Arab people.

The stirrings of debate during the 1990s ended prematurely, with a reaffirmation of the main ideas that had governed Middle East politics over the previous half century. Part of the reason for this was that the ruling elites in the Arab world and Iran, along with significant portions of the intelligentsia and the business community, feared change more than they did the status quo. Looking at regime changes in countries such as the Soviet Union, Romania, and Yugoslavia—symbols of liberation in the West—many Arabs saw chaos, ethnic strife, and the destruction of the old privileged classes (with whom Arab elites identified). In addition, existing doctrines, world-views, and propaganda lines remained effective in the Arab world, thereby hindering the momentum for change.

A pro-democracy movement did come into existence, but it remained small in every country except Lebanon and Iran. Once again, the notion that militant Arab nationalism was still an ideal—and that its lack of success was not due to internal shortcomings but rather to the machinations of the United States and Israel—remained widespread. As in the past, extremists were allowed to set the region's rhetorical tone, permissible limits, and agenda. In every Arab country radical Islamists constituted the main opposition group, the alternative to the existing system. While the ranks of pro-democracy moderates grew somewhat, the Arab nationalist regimes stayed in power and the Islamists became even stronger.

The following sections provide a brief review of specific areas where progress had been anticipated in 1991, and why that progress failed to materialize.

Turmoil in Iraq

In 1991 it was hoped that international sanctions would ensure that the Iraqi government either behaved more moderately or fell. Specifically, the international community sought to ensure that Iraq give up all weapons of mass destruction (chemical, biological, and nuclear weapons), a condition Iraq accepted after the Gulf War. Economic sanctions were to remain in place until United Nations weapons inspectors determined that Iraq had fully complied with its disarmament obligations.

While the sanctions took an awful toll on the Iraqi people, they neither drove Saddam from power nor caused him to cooperate fully with the

United Nations weapons inspectors examine shells containing mustard gas, near Fallujah, Iraq, 1991.

weapons inspectors. With the help of corrupt U.N. officials and foreign governments, Saddam managed to divert funds from oil sales—funds that were supposed to be used to buy food for the Iraqi people—to purchase arms and import luxury items. In this way he kept his armed forces and Baath Party political elites—the base of support for his regime—satisfied. With regard to Iraq's disarmament obligations, Saddam's government developed a strategy of concealment, sabotage, and non-cooperation designed to thwart the inspectors. By 2000 the sanctions program appeared to be faltering, and Saddam remained defiant.

The assertion that Iraq continued to possess weapons of mass destruction—which turned out to be incorrect—was offered as a justification for one of the most controversial decisions in U.S. history. In March 2003 the administration of President George W. Bush ordered an invasion of Iraq. Saddam Hussein's regime was quickly toppled, and with relatively minimal casualties. But maintaining order and setting up a stable government to replace the old regime proved another matter entirely.

Members of the former Iraqi army and Baath Party launched a bloody insurgency against the American and allied forces now occupying the country. Horrific violence between Iraq's minority Sunni Arab community (which had enjoyed power and privilege under Saddam) and its majority Shia community (which had been repressed, often brutally, by the old regime) eventually ignited a civil war. And radical Islamists from foreign countries flocked to Iraq to wage a jihad against the American forces. By the summer of 2007, more than four years after the invasion, there seemed little prospect that the violence might be quelled in the foreseeable future.

Many people in Iraq—and some in the wider Arab world—had welcomed the overthrow of Saddam. But as the country devolved into chaos and seemingly endless violence in the ensuing years, support for the U.S. action largely disappeared. Arab nationalists and Islamists began to portray Saddam—a horribly repressive dictator who had caused the deaths of hundreds of thousands of Arabs and Muslims—as a heroic champion brought

In Baghdad, a jubilant crowd watches as a statue of Saddam Hussein is pulled down, April 9, 2003. Although American forces toppled Saddam's regime with relative ease, they were unable to bring stability to Iraq.

down by imperialism. Nationalists and Islamists alike cheered on the insurgents and claimed that America was trying to steal Iraq's oil, enslave Arabs, and destroy Islam.

For leaders of other Arab states, events in Iraq serve as justification for maintaining the status quo. Reforms that are too deep or too quick, they say, could unleash the same kind of chaos and sectarian violence that Iraq has suffered. Better to have a less open but more stable (that is, authoritarian) society than to risk such an outcome.

Islamism Mutates

Although radical Islamists failed in their revolutionary efforts during the 1990s, this did not make them give up. Following the experience of the Iranian Revolution, Islamist groups gave precedence to overthrowing the regimes in their own countries. This required them to attack, fight, and kill fellow Muslims—which did not enhance their popularity among their co-religionists, who often viewed radical Islamists as members of a cult or as heretics. By the end of the decade, the Islamist strategy of domestic terrorism as a road to revolution had clearly failed.

Evaluating this situation, some Islamists began to propose a different course. The alternative to the Iranian model was the Afghan model. In Afghanistan during the 1980s, Islamists from around the world joined Afghan Muslims seeking to drive out Soviet forces that had invaded and occupied the country in December 1979. Their effort was immensely popular in the Muslim world, and it ultimately succeeded: the last Soviet soldiers withdrew from Afghanistan in early 1989. In the ensuing civil war, an extremely conservative Islamist group, the Taliban, gained control of most of the country by 1996. In its enforcement of a draconian form of Sharia, the Taliban met the approval of Islamists worldwide, many of whom considered Afghanistan the second truly Islamic state of modern times (after Iran).

Islamist theorists also noted that groups actively fighting against Israel—the Lebanon-based Hezbollah and the Palestinian groups Hamas and Islamic Jihad—were popular both among people in their own lands and among Muslims elsewhere. This led to the jihadist strategy of Osama bin Laden and his followers. Instead of putting the priority on attacking and overthrowing Arab regimes, bin Laden believed that Islamists should focus on killing Christians and Jews, Westerners and Israelis. Also, instead of purely local movements within each country, bin Laden created a federation of revolutionary groups—a kind of Islamist international.

Afghanistan's Taliban regime, which assumed power in 1996, instituted a draconian form of Sharia. Here an offender is publicly hanged in Kabul.

Bin Laden's organization, al-Qaeda, shocked the United States and galvanized the radical Islamist world by killing about 3,000 Americans in the coordinated terrorist attacks of September 11, 2001. Radical Islamism, it

Before striking on U.S. soil on September 11, 2001, Islamist terrorists conducted a series of attacks against American targets in the Middle East. (Above) Nineteen U.S. servicemen were killed in June 1996 when a massive truck bomb destroyed the Khobar Towers apartment complex in Dhahran, Saudi Arabia. (Opposite page) An explosives-laden dinghy attacked the USS *Cole* in the port of Aden, Yemen, producing the hole that is visible at the water line near the middle of the ship in this photo. The October 12, 2000, attack killed 17 American sailors.

appeared, had transcended almost a quarter century of failure to overthrow Arab regimes after Iran's revolution; the battle had been taken to the United States, which the Islamists saw as supporting the corrupt and impious Arab governments they loathed.

In 2000, in the face of continual attacks by Hezbollah fighters, Israeli forces pulled out of the buffer zone Israel had established in southern Lebanon 18 years earlier. This apparent victory of Hezbollah over Israel was taken as proof of the idea that a guerrilla or terrorist force would inevitably triumph over a militarily stronger opponent. Arafat's turn toward violence in the year 2000 let Hamas and Islamic Jihad again argue persuasively that their path was the only proper one. The great "success" of Osama bin Laden in striking at the United States in September 2001 seemed to show that this was an ideology that produced the real fighters, who would ultimately triumph while the Arab regimes stood by and did nothing.

Pursued by a U.S.-led war on terrorism, forced to flee Afghanistan, and somewhat intoxicated by their September 11 "victory," however, the jihadists moved back to their revolutionary efforts in the Arab world. Although able to set off a great deal of violence, especially in Saudi Arabia and Iraq, the jihadists enjoyed no

real successes. Nevertheless, not only did the movement survive but its popularity also rose, for fighting the infidel enemy. Many conservative-traditionalist Muslims, including establishment clerics, increasingly sounded like Islamists.

Yet even this was not all. More successful than the jihadists were the various branches of the Muslim Brotherhood. In Egypt and Syria (Muslim Brotherhood), Jordan (Islamic Salvation Front), and among the Palestinians (Hamas), Brotherhood forces organized successfully. In all those places except Syria, they were also able to take advantage of elections to build their base of support. The January 2006 electoral victory of Hamas over the Palestinian nationalists seemed to show the efficacy of this new approach.

Thus, radical Islamist views remained at least as popular in the early 21st century as they had been a decade earlier, and perhaps even more so. Especially widely accepted was the new worldview promoted by the Islamists. The Christians and Jews, America and Europe, as well as Israel were all aggressors trying to destroy Islam. In self-defense, Muslims would wage jihad and be given the victory by God. Arab nationalists were ineffective, while Arab liberals were actually Western agents. Radical Islamism had become what communism and fascism had been in Europe during the 20th century: a comprehensive doctrine that blamed all problems on scapegoats and promised a utopia in the near future. Even as the movement failed to win political victories, it conquered millions of minds throughout the Arab world.

The Unsolved Conflict

In 1991 the Palestinians, too, were at the low point of their fortunes. Hundreds of Palestinians had died in the *intifada*—an uprising against Israeli occupation in the West Bank and Gaza Strip, which began in 1987. Saddam Hussein, a hero to many Palestinians and a financial supporter of the PLO, had been defeated. Arab states were also less willing to help their Palestinian brethren, and the cutoff of aid from Kuwait and Saudi Arabia had produced a financial crisis in the PLO. Moreover, around 350,000 Palestinian refugees had been forced out of Kuwait in the aftermath of the Gulf War. The Soviet Union was in its last throes, depriving the Palestinians of another important ally and leaving the United States—which the PLO had viewed as its arch-enemy—the world's sole superpower. Israel appeared stronger than ever. If ever there was a time for the Palestinians to make a compromise peace, recognizing that they could not achieve their maximal goals, the 1990s seemed to be that time.

Thus there were great expectations that the Palestinians, Syrians, and others would make peace with Israel. This seemed to be the pattern for how other conflicts were settled: a period of passionate hatred gave way to pragmatic solutions. Surely if offered a state—not to mention many billions of dollars in refugee compensation—Yasir Arafat would accept. After so many decades of struggle, bloodshed, and suffering—with no sign of any possible total victory through force—the alternative seemed unthinkable. This conclusion was reinforced by the 1991 Madrid Conference, which was hosted by Spain and cosponsored by the United States and the Soviet Union; follow-up negotiations in Washington, D.C.; and a peace agreement between Israel and the PLO, dubbed the Oslo accords, which was reached in 1993. However, while the Oslo accords (officially the "Declaration of Principles on Interim Self-Government Arrangements") led to the establishment of the Palestinian

Authority, a Palestinian body charged with administering the West Bank and Gaza Strip, it put off many contentious issues until final-status talks to be held five years after the implementation of the Oslo accords' terms.

In 1994 Jordan and Israel concluded a comprehensive peace agreement. Syria and the Palestinians, however, did not come to terms with Israel for a full peace. The history of the Syria-Israel and Palestinian-Israel peace

Israeli prime minister Ehud Barak (left) and PLO chairman Yasir Arafat (right) appear grim during a July 2000 peace summit hosted by President Bill Clinton in Camp David, Maryland. Soon after the peace talks collapsed, a new round of violence erupted in the Israeli-occupied West Bank.

processes is very complex. Talks between Syria and Israel bogged down in 1996. In July 2000 U.S. president Bill Clinton hosted a summit at the presidential retreat in Camp David, Maryland, between Yasir Arafat and Israeli prime minister Ehud Barak. The hope was that issues standing in the way of a final-status agreement—such as permanent borders between Israel and the proposed Palestinian state; control of Jerusalem, which has deep religious significance for Jews and Muslims, as well as Christians; and the right of return of Palestinian refugees—could be resolved. By most accounts, Barak made significant concessions, but Arafat balked, and the summit broke up with no agreement.

Many factors may have contributed to the failure of Syria and the Palestinians to reach a full peace agreement with Israel, including the Arab leaders' inability or unwillingness to go against public opinion in their constituencies, a belief that total victory for their side was inevitable, overwhelming suspicion of Israel, or—especially in the case of Arafat—simple intransigence. Yet beyond these factors, arguably, was one more that stood at the center of Arab politics: the Arab-Israeli conflict was too useful a political tool for the regimes to abandon. If peace were to be made, this tool, which provided a scapegoat and distraction from their failures, would be lost to Arab politicians. Demands for democracy, economic reform, and political change could be expected to multiply, threatening the power of entrenched Arab regimes. At the same time, many people—especially the Islamists—would argue that peace with Israel was tantamount to treason, and such an argument might hold sway among the masses. Again, the power of old regimes could be seriously threatened.

If the Arab states could keep the conflict as a propaganda instrument without actually having to fight Israel, the status quo was all the more attractive. As for the Islamists themselves, the conflict was the main proof of the perfidy of the West, the satanic nature of Israel, and the inability of the nationalists to gain victory.

The bottom line was that the Palestinians and Syrians proved unable to meet the challenge of achieving a compromise peace with Israel—even one that met most of their demands—and other Arab states would not shake loose from giving them veto power in ending the conflict. The conclusion the Arab world seemed to draw from this experience was not a need for greater compromise and conciliation but instead a duty to strive for more effective violence, mobilization, and steadfastness to old demands.

By the end of the year 2000, Arab attitudes had reverted to those of 20 years earlier. Israel was demonized to astounding levels, and a belief in the possibility of total victory returned in the minds of a new generation who had not experienced the frustrations and defeats of the past.

The Palestinian Authority, which since its inception had been dominated by nationalists—specifically, Yasir Arafat's Fatah wing of the PLO—earned a reputation for corruption and incompetence. By 2006 Palestinians were thoroughly disillusioned with Fatah. In January elections for the Palestinian Authority parliament, voters overwhelmingly cast their ballots for Hamas. This choice was made easier by the fact that aside from Hamas's emphasis on Islamism, there was no real difference between its program and the one put forward by the Fatah nationalists.

Supporters of Hamas celebrate the radical Islamist group's victory in January 2006 elections for the Palestinian Authority parliament.

It was easy for the Arab masses to believe—as their leaders and media told them daily—that only cowardice and treason could prevent Israel's elimination or encourage peaceful compromise with such a vile entity. Arab-Israeli peace, and certainly Palestinian-Israeli peace, was as far away as ever before.

Iran: Radicalism Revisited

When it came to Iran, the 1990s seemed to show the regime on the defensive. Reformers won election after election. In 1997, by an overwhelming majority,

Above: Iranian president Mohammad Khatami (right), a moderate reformer, was unable to overcome the power of Supreme Leader Ayatollah Ali Khamenei (left) and Iran's other mullahs. Opposite page: Mahmoud Ahmadinejad, who replaced Khatami in 2005, was an extreme hard-liner.

voters gave the presidency to Mohammad Khatami, a moderate who promised change. Khatami easily won reelection in 2001.

If it was inevitable that revolutions mellowed and either moderated or lost popular support, Iran's future seemed clear. Yet Khatami and the liberal-dominated parliament accomplished little, partly because of the veto power hard-line institutions hold under Iran's political system. Khatami would not challenge the revolution, and the outmaneuvered reform movement fell apart. Disillusioned, many Iranians returned to long habits of political passivity.

Having lost patience with the reformists' challenge, Iran's clerical establishment changed the rules for the 2005 elections. With voter participation falling and disgust with the establishment still manifest, the regime-backed candidate lost to an even more extreme hard-liner, Mahmoud Ahmadinejad. Ahmadinejad proceeded to amaze and anger the world with his belligerent and outlandish statements. Meanwhile, Iran was driving steadily toward acquiring nuclear weapons. Iran also strove to infiltrate and gain influence in post-Saddam Iraq. Rather than moderating, the Iranian Revolution appeared to be growing more extreme, more dangerous, and more entrenched than it had been in the early 1990s.

Attitudes Toward the United States

While the United States was the world's sole superpower, events of the 1990s and after showed its limited power to dictate changes in the Middle East. U.S. policy ultimately failed to moderate Iranian behavior, resolve the Arab-Israeli conflict, eliminate terrorism, or promote substantive reform.

In many cases—especially in the aftermath of the September 11, 2001, terrorist attacks—regimes in the Middle East seemed more deferential to U.S. goals and policies, but their agendas diverged in critical ways from that of the United States. Thus, the war against terrorism provided opportunities to limit freedoms in the name of stability or to repress opposition groups, even when those groups did not espouse terrorism. Arab rulers also claimed to be pursuing democratization to defuse American pressure or criticism over that issue.

At the same time, Arab regimes, media, and intellectuals—along with their Islamist rival counterparts—developed a systematic interpretation of the United States in order to discredit it among their own people. The United States was said to be the leader of a massive Christian-Jewish conspiracy to destroy the Arabs and Islam. Every American action was also counted as further proof of its treachery. This was understandable on the part of the radical regimes, which wanted to isolate the moderates in their midst and deny them a protector. Yet often the moderates also refused to say anything positive about the United States.

After the September 11 attacks, state-controlled media in countries nominally allied with the United States—including Saudi Arabia and Egypt—were overwhelmingly hostile toward America. They often focused on complaints about U.S. policy (notably toward Israel) while ignoring American aid to Arab states and peoples. (Egypt, for example, had been the second-largest recipient of U.S. foreign aid since 1979, getting about $2 billion annually.) The U.S. war in Iraq was extremely unpopular in the Arab world, where it was depicted as proof of American imperialism and even of American intentions to destroy Islam. Even without the Iraq War, however, many Arab regimes would have harshly criticized the United States at home, as they did for decades before the war. Thus, while U.S. superiority in power could not be ignored, it could be deflected and reduced as a factor pushing for domestic change.

The newsroom of Al Jazeera, a Qatar-based satellite news network whose coverage often includes an Islamist perspective.

The Failure of Democratization

The newest feature in the Arab world was the campaign for democratization. Liberals appeared—albeit often in small numbers—advocating human rights, free elections, and civil society. U.S. support for these changes helped put them on the Arab agenda, yet activists in Arab countries remained minority voices. The regimes maneuvered but generally gave little or nothing to their subjects. Elections were fixed as always, perhaps with the rulers taking a slightly smaller majority, or the main gains went to the Islamists rather than the liberals.

Thus, while the drive for liberalization might be an important trend in the long run, it changed little immediately. There were some exceptions—stronger parliaments in Bahrain and Kuwait, women's suffrage in Kuwait, a family law giving more rights to women in Morocco, and perhaps most notably the Lebanese civic revolt against Syrian occupation. Still, the results were far less than even the most staid moderate would have expected in 1991.

Failure of Development Reform

After 1991 many Arab economies stagnated, leading to deteriorating living conditions for citizens. Yet aside from certain relatively minor changes made by some of the smaller Gulf states—notably the United Arab Emirates—no Arab country overhauled its economic policies. Beginning around 2003, however, higher prices for crude oil put billions of additional dollars into the treasuries of oil-producing states, raising living standards in Saudi Arabia and a few other places. Still, restrictive laws, political instability, sporadic violence, and institutional weaknesses in sectors such as banking continued to limit economic growth.

In 1999 the *Star*, a Jordanian weekly newspaper, published this gloomy assessment of the region's prospects:

> The Middle East is slipping behind in the . . . competition for markets and capital. States have interfered arbitrarily and ineffectively too often, created lopsided, uncompetitive state sectors, extended subsidies and entitlements which are difficult

to withdraw or reduce, and depend too much on rising oil revenues. Economies are not diversified enough or integrated regionally. Population growth has raised a host of problems for states, from education and job creation to the need to trim subsidies and welfare systems. Most of the remedies for a more efficient private sector have important political implications, notably more transparency and greater rule of law.

In the midst of these difficulties and failures, many people concluded that the Arab states and Iran had to make major shifts in their political and economic systems in order to avoid decades of continued crisis, or possibly even the collapse of several countries in the region.

That was not exactly the conclusion of the Middle East's rulers or of Islamists. Fundamental change in the form of democracy and free-market economics, in their view, was undesirable. Such change might fuel instability, bringing suffering to everyone—and, of course, threatening the power and wealth of the privileged.

Instead of committing to a course that might produce tangible material benefits for a broad section of society, populist regimes sought to satisfy their people with economic subsidies and ideological fulfillment. As Saddam Hussein had assured his people, "If those who surpass you in material things and appearances outrun you, do not follow them. Choose your own honorable path. . . . Your clinging to these principles will be deeper in effect, firmer in stand and higher in position."

(Opposite) American soldiers on patrol in Iraq. (Right) An Iraqi man casts his vote in December 2005 parliamentary elections. The U.S. goal of creating a stable, functioning democracy in Iraq has proved elusive.

5 *Battle for the Future*

$\mathcal{T}$he question of which leaders and, more important, what kind of political system will govern the Arab world holds enormous significance for the future of the Middle East. In fact, given the region's vast reserves of petroleum and its central importance for Muslims—including Islamic extremists bent on driving out Western and other foreign cultural influences—the direction the Middle East takes will have dramatic repercussions for the entire world.

Essentially, there are three blueprints for the Middle East's future. They are the status quo, sustained by appeals to pan-Arab nationalism; political Islamism; and reform along liberal democratic lines.

59

The Status Quo

With few exceptions, radical pan-Arab nationalism has been the dominant ideology throughout the Arab world during the last half century. In a few instances—most notably the establishment of the United Arab Republic (UAR) in 1958—a measure of progress was made toward the central goal of Pan-Arabism: the political unification of all Arab lands into a single Arab state. But such progress was modest, and it was fleeting—the UAR, a union of Egypt and Syria, broke up in little more than three years. Today it is safe to say that very few Arab leaders and intellectuals, if any, favor the political unification of all Arab countries. Yet Arab regimes continue to pay lip service to the idea that Arab unity is the most important political virtue, and they frequently cloak themselves in the mantle of defender of the Arab people or of the Muslim faith.

By invoking the spirit of pan-Arab nationalism in this manner, repressive regimes seek legitimacy. They also seek to deflect criticism of their poor performance. The United States, the West in general, and Israel are blamed for the problems in Arab societies, and the struggle against these outside forces is portrayed as the solution.

Yet the failure of Arab nationalism to deliver on its key promises, after a half century as the Arab world's dominant ideology, is obvious. Israel has not been destroyed. U.S. and Western influences have not been expelled. Arab states have not achieved rapid economic growth, and Arab peoples remain divided.

Nevertheless, the Arab regimes—both traditionalist monarchies and military-based dictatorships—have proved remarkably adept at fending off

A truckload of Hamas gunmen patrols the Gaza Strip, June 17, 2007. Hamas had earlier gained control of Gaza after fighting with the other dominant Palestinian faction, Fatah. With the Hamas-Fatah dispute threatening to spread to the West Bank, Palestinian Authority president Mahmoud Abbas quickly swore in an emergency government.

internal challenges, and virtually immune to reform. Central to this is their willingness to subordinate all institutions and state resources to the goal of holding on to power, and to use all available tools of persuasion. These include repression, corruption, patronage, control of the economy and media, and careful supervision of the armed forces.

Despite all their efforts, Arab regimes have been unable to eliminate dissatisfaction with the status quo. In fact, the very militancy and bluster of the Arab nationalist rhetoric those regimes have employed encourages discontent, because the promises and the reality are so divergent.

Islamism

Radical political Islamism offers an alternative to the status quo, and it has grown to be the main opposition movement in every Arab country. Significantly, Islamism accepts the basic premises of Arab nationalism but merely wants to substitute a different ideological driving force. For the Islamists, the problems afflicting their societies are not the result of dictatorial rule or extremism per se. Rather, they are due to the corrupting effect of external ideas and influences and the machinations of foreign enemies. The regimes' most glaring shortcoming, Islamists maintain, lies in their failure to fight these forces harder (or, in many cases, their outright embrace of illicit influences). The prescription for healing Arab societies is encapsulated in a popular Islamist slogan: "Islam is the solution." In other words, Islam (or, more accurately, the particular form of Islam endorsed by the specific Islamist group in question) should be adopted as the basis for all political, social, and personal life. When it is, the Islamists say, all the benefits promised but not produced by Arab nationalism will be obtained. In short, Islam is the way to utopia.

While this message holds tremendous emotional appeal, it is by no means apparent that Islamism will triumph in the Middle East—and not simply because of the existing regimes' skill at maintaining power through repression and co-optation. Many pious Muslims look at political Islamism as a controversial or even heretical way of interpreting their religion. Despite recent electoral gains in countries such as Egypt and Lebanon, as well as in the Palestinian territories, Islamists appear a long way from gaining control of any Arab state, whether through elections or through revolutions. Their efforts to transform Arab societies will be one of the defining dramas of the coming years.

Liberal Reform

The Gulf War of 1991, as well as U.S. pressure on Middle Eastern governments to democratize following the terrorist attacks of September 11, 2001, created an opportunity for Arabs who sought to reform their societies along liberal democratic lines. These reformers offered an entirely different vision of the Middle East's future. They sought to address their countries' internal problems, and they championed solutions that have often worked well, if not perfectly, elsewhere in the world. Such solutions include more democracy; greater transparency and accountability in government; a more robust civil society; less state control of economies and a greater reliance on free markets; a free press; and a more scrupulous observance of human rights.

In some countries, reformers made modest gains. Kuwait, for example, gave women the right to vote and to seek office (though in the 2006 elections, no female candidates won a seat in the country's 50-member parliament). In Lebanon, massive popular demonstrations in 2005 ended Syria's 29-year military occupation and caused the pro-Syria government to fall. Beginning in late 2001 Egypt permitted a greater degree of free speech, but within two years the government had cracked down hard on dissenters.

Lebanese demonstrators in Beirut's Martyrs Square call for the withdrawal of Syrian troops from their country, March 2, 2005. Ultimately the Syrian army did pull out after a 29-year occupation.

Reformers, despite some successes, remain weak. And by 2007, some Arab rulers appeared inclined to suspend the small concessions they had earlier made. Reformers face a host of difficulties. In many countries they are vulnerable to being characterized as enemies of tradition or as lackeys of the West. Other critics paint them as irresponsible and naive dreamers whose ideas could lead to the collapse of Arab societies or violent anarchy.

Yet while their prospects for effecting fundamental change may be minuscule in the short term, they should not be discounted in the long term. Democracy did not develop overnight—in America, Europe, or anywhere else. Nor was the road to Western-style liberal societies a straight one. During the 20th century, at a time when the progress of European civilization seemed secure, Europe nurtured the unimaginable horrors of fascism and communism. It is by no means certain that moderation, pragmatism, and democracy will prevail over extremism, violence, and tyranny in the Middle East. But if they do, the process is likely to take a very long time.

A Kuwaiti woman casts her vote during June 2006 parliamentary elections.

1990: On August 2, Iraq's army invades and occupies Kuwait. Over the following weeks and months, a U.S.-led military coalition is assembled to reverse Iraq's aggression by force if necessary.

1991: On January 17, two days after the expiration of a U.N.-established deadline for Iraq to completely withdraw from Kuwait or face military action, U.S. forces and their coalition allies launch massive air and missile attacks on targets in Kuwait and Iraq, marking the beginning of the Gulf War. On February 28, after 100 hours of ground fighting during which Iraqi forces are routed, the coalition institutes a cease-fire.

In April, Saudi dissident Osama bin Laden, founder of the Islamist terrorist group al-Qaeda, flees Saudi Arabia after being confined to Jeddah for his opposition to the Saudi alliance with the United States.

In November, an international peace conference aimed at ending the Arab-Israeli conflict meets in Madrid. This marks the first time that several Arab states—including Syria and Saudi Arabia—have negotiated with Israel.

In December, an Islamist party in Algeria, the Islamic Salvation Front (FIS), wins the first round of parliamentary elections and is poised to obtain a majority in the second round when the Algerian military nullifies the victory, forces the president to resign, and bans the FIS. A more radical group, the Armed Islamic Group (GIA), breaks from the FIS to wage an armed struggle for an Islamist state. Over the next six years, as many as 100,000 Algerians will be killed in the fighting.

1992: On April 18, the Communist government in Afghanistan is overthrown as Islamic Afghan guerrilla leaders take control of the capital, Kabul, and declare the Islamic State of Afghanistan. Within the country, Islamist groups struggle for power.

On June 10, members of al-Gama'a al-Islamiyya assassinate Faraj Foda, a prominent Egyptian writer known for his criticism of Islamist extremism. At the trial of Foda's killers, Sheikh Muhammad al-Ghazali, a cleric at al-Azhar, the prestigious institution of Islamic teaching, declares that anyone who resists Islamic law is an apostate and may be killed.

On June 29, Algeria's head of state Mohamed Boudiaf is assassinated by a bodyguard with suspected Islamist ties.

In November, Egyptian president Hosni Mubarak announces that some 40,000 private mosques, some of which are believed to be the breeding ground for terrorists, will be taken under government control. The edict is announced only days after a mosque in Assiut calls on its members to join an armed struggle against the central government and condemns Christians and Jews as a "common enemy."

1993: On September 13, during a ceremony at the White House, Israeli prime minister Yitzhak Rabin and PLO chairman Yasir Arafat sign the Oslo accords, in which the PLO vows to disavow violence and recognize Israel, and Israel agrees to a phased withdrawal from the West Bank and Gaza and the creation of a Palestinian self-governing entity. The agreement mandates a series of negotiations leading to a comprehensive resolution of all issues within five years of the start of implementation.

1994: On July 1, Arafat enters the Gaza Strip for the first time in 27 years to set up a ruling entity, called the Palestinian Authority. The Palestinian Authority, which at this stage includes the entire Gaza Strip and the West Bank town of Jericho, will administer the areas turned over to Arafat's rule. A primary responsibility will be to prevent terrorism against Israelis.

1995: On June 26, the Islamic Group unsuccessfully attempts to assassinate Egyptian president Hosni Mubarak in Addis Ababa, Ethiopia.

On September 28, the so-called Oslo 2 agreement is signed, providing for Israeli withdrawal from all West Bank towns except Hebron and their turnover to the Palestinian Authority's rule.

On November 4, Israeli prime minister Yitzhak Rabin is assassinated by a right-wing Israeli law school student who wants to stop the peace process with the Palestinians.

1996: In response to U.S. pressure and the threat of U.N. sanctions, Sudan expels Osama bin Laden, who takes refuge in Afghanistan. On August 23, he issues a "declaration of war" against Christians and Jews throughout the world.

On September 26, the Taliban militia, which had been fighting a civil war in Afghanistan, captures Kabul and establishes the Islamic Emirate of Afghanistan. The Taliban will host training bases for Islamist radicals from around the world.

1997: On November 17, Islamic Group gunmen shoot and kill 62 people, including 58 tourists, and wound 26 others at a popular Egyptian tourist site, the Hatshepsut Temple in the Valley of the Kings near Luxor.

1998: On February 23, bin Laden announces the creation of a new alliance of terrorist organizations, the "International Islamic Front for Jihad Against the Jews and Crusaders" and says it is the duty of all observant Muslims to kill Americans, including civilians.

2000: In June, Syrian dictator Hafez al-Assad dies and is replaced as the country's ruler by his son Bashar.

In July, Yasir Arafat and Israeli prime minister Ehud Barak meet at Camp David, Maryland, for peace negotiations mediated by U.S. president Bill

Clinton. The talks collapse when Arafat rejects the offer of an independent Palestinian state in all of the Gaza Strip and most of the West Bank and East Jerusalem and financial compensation for refugees.

2001: On September 11, al-Qaeda terrorists hijack four U.S. jetliners, crashing two into the World Trade Center and one into the Pentagon; the fourth, believed to be headed for the White House or the Capitol, crashes into a field in western Pennsylvania after a struggle between passengers and the hijackers. About 3,000 people are killed in the attacks.

In October, U.S. and British forces attack Afghanistan, whose Taliban regime harbors bin Laden and other al-Qaeda members.

On November 13, Taliban fighters abandon Kabul, the Afghan capital.

2003: In March, U.S. forces—joined by forces from the United Kingdom and other coalition partners—attack Iraq. Within three weeks, the regime of Saddam Hussein has been toppled. However, Iraq is soon gripped by deadly violence between the country's Sunni and Shia communities, an insurgency by former soldiers in the Iraqi army and other Saddam loyalists, and attacks by foreign Islamist fighters.

2005: In January, Iraq holds elections to choose an assembly that will write a new constitution.

On February 14, Rafiq Hariri, Lebanon's former prime minister, is assassinated in Beirut, apparently by Syrian agents.

In April, following massive demonstrations demanding their withdrawal, Syrian troops pull out of Lebanon after 29 years in the country.

In August, Israeli forces withdraw from all of the Gaza Strip and part of the West Bank.

In December, under the new Iraqi constitution, elections are held to choose a government.

2006: In January elections for the Palestinian parliament, Hamas wins a big victory; the Islamist group also achieves victories several months earlier in local elections.

2007: In June fighting between Hamas and Fatah leaves Hamas in control of Gaza.

annex—to incorporate new territory within a larger state.

Cold War—the worldwide political and ideological struggle between the United States and the Soviet Union, which began after World War II and lasted until the collapse of the Soviet Union in 1991.

civil society—the sum total of institutions, organizations, and groups promoting social and civic causes in a country (for example, human rights groups, labor unions, arts foundations) that are not funded or controlled by the government or business interests.

elites—the socially, economically, and politically privileged in a society.

emirate—a state ruled by a Muslim leader known as an emir.

gross domestic product (GDP)—the total value of goods and services produced in a one-year period (considered a good measure of the overall size of a country's economy).

GDP per capita—the total value of goods and services produced by a country's economy in a one-year period, divided by the country's population (considered a good measure of national prosperity).

ideology—a system of beliefs, values, and ideas forming the basis of a social, economic, or political philosophy.

intelligentsia—the most educated and intelligent members of a society; the intellectual elite.

Islamist—a Muslim who advocates the reformation of society and government in accordance with Islamic laws and principles.

jihad—a "holy war" waged by Muslims on behalf of Islam.

jihadism—adherence to the idea that Muslims should carry out a war against un-Islamic groups and ideas, especially Westerners and Western liberal culture.

nationalism—the belief that shared ethnicity, language, and history should form the basis for political organization; the desire of people with a common culture to have their own state.

Pan-Arabism—a movement seeking to unite all Arab peoples into a single state.

Sharia—Islamic law.

Atkinson, Rick. *Crusade: The Untold Story of the Persian Gulf War*. New York: Houghton Mifflin, 1993.

Bergen, Peter. *Holy War, Inc.: Inside the Secret War of Osama bin Laden*. New York: Free Press, 2002.

Chayes, Sarah. *The Punishment of Virtue: Inside Afghanistan After the Taliban*. New York: Penguin, 2006.

Ginat, Joseph, et al., eds. *The Middle East Peace Process: Vision Versus Reality*. Norman: University of Oklahoma Press, 2002.

Ricks, Thomas E. *Fiasco: The American Military Adventure in Iraq*. New York: Penguin, 2006.

http://meria.idc.ac.il/journal/index/journalindex.html

The *Middle East Review of International Affairs (MERIA) Journal* offers scholarly articles on a wide variety of topics affecting the region and the world.

http://www.pbs.org/wgbh/pages/frontline/gulf/

The companion website for the PBS *Frontline* documentary *The Gulf War* includes interviews with key decision makers, maps, a chronology, and accounts of soldiers' experiences during the conflict.

http://www.yale.edu/lawweb/avalon/mideast/isrplo.htm

Text of the 1993 peace agreement between Israel and the Palestine Liberation Organization.

http://www.columbia.edu/cu/lweb/indiv/mideast/cuvlm/

The Middle East Studies Internet Resources site, maintained by Columbia University Libraries, contains links to a broad array of sources providing geographic, political, cultural, and historical information.

Numbers in ***bold italic*** refer to captions.

Contributors

Barry Rubin is director of the Global Research in International Affairs (GLORIA) Center of the Interdisciplinary University. He is editor of the *Middle East Review of International Affairs (MERIA) Journal.*

Picture Credits